the who, what, when, where, how & why of saving sex for marriage

Beth Steury

Copyright © 2018 Beth Steury

All rights reserved.

Life Matters Publishing

ISBN: 978-0-9991970-2-8

DEDICATION

*To anyone and everyone,
guys and girls alike,
young and old and in between,
virgin or not.
Because YOU matter.*

CONTENTS

1	What's the big deal?	1
2	WHO's got your back?	5
3	WHO can you trust?	9
4	WHAT if it's already too late?	13
5	But WHEN? I want to . . . NOW!	17
6	Yep, the WHERE matters too	23
7	WHERE does your mind hang-out?	27
8	HOW far is too far?	31
9	HOW? No back-up plan	37
10	WHY save sex for marriage?	41
11	WHY? Do you know where babies come from?	45
12	WHY? The facts and fiction about STDs	49
13	WHY wait? It's all about the bonding	53

1

WHAT's the big deal?

I'm only 13
　　　or 17
　　　　　or 21.

I'm not seeing anyone now…
　　…never been in a relationship.
　　　　…no plans to date anytime soon.
I'm focused on things other than the opposite sex.
　　…like finishing high school

...hanging with my friends

...choosing a college

...getting my career going

...living my life

Or maybe you're already in a relationship—part of a committed couple.

"My boyfriend and I? Well, all we do is kiss.

Sex . . . that's not what we're about.

It's never been an issue for us."

"Me and my girl? We respect each other.

We're not that physical anyway.

I'm not worried."

There's a hundred reasons people give for not making a personal decision about sex. They insist now's not the time to bother with signing a pledge or to worry about making a commitment or keeping a promise.

"Hey, I'll figure it out when I need to—when it becomes an issue."

Not a good idea.

The truth is there'll never be a better time than right now.

Spur of the moment decisions are almost always wrong. Especially if those decisions take place in the arms of someone you like a lot—maybe even love.

If you wait until the question of having sex is already an "issue", the chances of making a wise decision are slim. It's so much harder to make good choices in the heat of a passionate moment.

Do yourself a huge favor. Settle the question now. Choose to save sex for marriage. Before the issue is staring you in the face, make a decision to wait for sex.

Because YOU are worth waiting for.

Even in this sex-crazed world, it's possible to save sex for marriage. It's all about paying attention to the

WHO

WHAT

WHEN

WHERE

HOW

and

WHY

of saving sex for marriage.

2

WHO's got your back?

It's a one size fits all kind of thing. You won't find ethnicity or age range circles to color in. And despite what you may have heard, there's no gender boxes to check either. Because none of those things come into play when you're considering having sex.

No matter who you are, where you live, what's in your past, saving sex for marriage is a win-win situation.

If you're saving your first sexual experience for the one you pledge your life to, ***you're making the best possible choice.***

If yours is a commitment to "renewed waiting", because you already had sex in the past, ***then you're*** *making a huge, positive investment in your future.*

Nothing is smarter than stopping something that puts you at risk physically, emotionally and mentally.

Even if you think you're doin' okay in the saving sex for marriage department, don't try to go it alone. Especially if yours is a commitment to "renewed waiting", you'll need lots of support and encouragement along the way.

We're not meant to live alone. Secluded islands may be awesome for a relaxing vacation, but in real life we need each other. Especially for the tough stuff. And saving sex for marriage definitely falls into that category.

Who in your life is tough enough to lay it on the line and not put up with your handy excuses or lame rationalizations?

Your best friend? Maybe but only if that person's commitment to waiting is at least as strong as yours. *If he or she wavers at all on the subject, they won't be much help to you.*

If you're lucky enough to have multiple like-minded friends, make a pact to have each other's back. There's strength and unity in numbers.

If you're comfortable discussing sex with Mom

and Dad, go for it. They haven't been married forever—they were teenagers once, too, you know. They can steer you toward decisions that will help rather than hurt your commitment to wait.

But sometimes it's easier to have gut-level chats about sex with someone who didn't have a role in your conception. Whether it's a teacher, a co-worker, a coach, a friend's parent, or your pastor, find someone you can talk to.

Prove to yourself and everyone else that this is a serious commitment by seeking a mentor/accountability kind of set-up with a trusted adult.

Look at the people in your life.

- Who will you feel comfortable with and allow to hold you to firm boundaries?
- Whose honest feedback will you really, really listen to?
- Whose tough-love attitude will keep you headed in the right direction?

Surround yourself with support and encouragement and accountability.

You CAN win the battle to protect or renew your virginity.

3

WHO can you trust?

You've decided to save sex or at least any more sexual experiences for your wedding night. ***Way to go. That's a decision you won't regret. I promise.***

But now you're looking around, wondering who you can trust with your no-sex commitment?

The last time I checked, no one wore t-shirts screen-printed with

"saving sex for marriage—looking for a like-minded guy"

or

"virgin groom looking for virgin bride".

Although maybe that's not a bad idea. Could

prevent a lot of grief and heart ache.

But really, how can you know who the "safe" girls and guys are? The ones who won't hassle you or make it harder than it already is to stay away from sex.

These eight strategies can help you navigate the choppy waters of waiting or "renewed waiting" without the aid of labeled apparel.

- ✓ ***Don't hide your commitment.*** Be open about your decision to save sex for marriage. "Open" doesn't mean you begin every sentence with *"Since I'm saving myself…"* What it does mean is don't fade into the background when the subject at lunch or in the locker room or at the game turns to sex. Admit your decision without judging the choice of others.

- ✓ **Girls,** pay attention to how you act and dress around guys, and everyone else for that matter. Excessive flirtiness and flaunting what you say you're saving for your future husband will attract the wrong kind of guy.

- ✓ **Guys,** show your respect for the female gender by treating girls the way you want guys to treat your little sister. If you slip into macho, cool dude, womanizing mode, you'll be sending out the wrong vibe.

- ✓ **Girls**, listen up when a guy talks, whatever the subject. His inner self—thoughts, motives, values—will seep out between the lines.

- ✓ **Guys**, pay attention to what she does and doesn't say about herself, her friends, and the male species.

- ✓ *Everyone*, hanging out in groups is a great way to learn more about that interesting guy or fascinating girl. Of course, make sure the group's agenda doesn't include pairing off or hooking up. Or the use of alcohol and drugs.

- ✓ ***Being friends first is always a good plan.*** Going out with someone you barely know can get you into trouble.

- ✓ ***Don't rush into "couple" status.*** The tug to express physical affection is always greater once you're "official".

It matters WHO you spend time with. It matters WHO you go out with. Because YOU are worth waiting for.

Beth Steury

4

"WHAT if it's already too late?"

"I already didn't wait," you say. "So it's too late to think about saving myself for my husband or wife."

"No use worrying about somethin' I can't change."

"Abstinence matters to those who haven't had sex, maybe. But not to someone like me."

If that's how you feel, you're not alone. Tons of people didn't wait and have convinced themselves that it's too late to choose a different path—to change their thinking, their ways, their values . . . whatever.

But it's not too late.

No, you can't "will" yourself to be a virgin again. It doesn't quite work that way. **But you can stop putting yourself at risk emotionally, physically, and mentally.** At any point you can say "no" to sex outside of a marriage commitment and choose "renewed waiting".

I already hear a chorus of voices crying out,

"But you don't understand!"

"I can't make a big deal about it now. We've been doin' it for a long time."

"She'll leave me if I say 'no' now."

"He loves me."

"We're getting married . . . next month, next year . . . someday."

But I do get it. If you're in a sexually active relationship, yeah, it will be tough to back things up. It will take determination and perseverance and guts—from both of you. Some sort of accountability set-up will be a must.

Tough, yes. Impossible, no. Not with the right encouragement and support.

Maybe you're not so much into relationships as

into hooking up or casual sex.

"Everyone knows I do it. It's expected."

"It's my business who and if I sleep with someone . . . or multiple someones."

"It's only sex. So what?"

Listen up—

"Casual" and "sex" were never meant to go together. NEVER EVER.

You may think you're getting sex without strings, but really you aren't. Even casual sex produces memories . . . that lead to feelings . . . that create ties. ***Because that's the way sex is supposed to work.***

If you're in a "committed" relationship, this is the time to dig deep into every part of the relationship— **except the physical.** Why?

Because the allure of sex will steal time and effort from the pursuit of getting to know each other on a deeper level.

The temptation to regularly put aside the exploring of goals, ideals, values and beliefs, in favor of exploring hard muscles and soft curves, will be huge. And you'll probably lose.

You deserve so much more than the momentary thrill of sex with no meaning, no commitment, no purpose.

The best sex you'll ever have is in a love-anchored, committed marriage.

And you deserve the best. Despite how much your past or your friends or your special someone tries to convince you otherwise.

Don't settle for anything less.

5

"But WHEN? I want to . . . now!"

Our pleasure-seeking, I-want-it-now (whatever "it" is) society sees absolutely no reason to wait for anything. **We want what we want, WHEN we want it. And that usually means now.**

Not getting what we want is worse than just about anything we can think of. We'll do almost anything to avoid it.

- ✓ break a promise to our self or someone else
- ✓ put aside long-held beliefs
- ✓ comprise on a moral issue
- ✓ even lie

Because that to-die-for helping of Death-By-Chocolate left us wanting more, we indulge in another hefty portion, ignoring the pricking of a conscience that's committed to portion control.

Because we cannot abide the thought of waiting until the money is in hand for that brand new, must-have video game or music download or basketball shoes or designer jeans, we buy on time, borrow, or in some other way over-extend ourselves. Then shut down the guilt from yet another unwise decision.

Because the allure of sex is soooo tempting . . . soooo strong . . . soooo promising, we can't possibly ignore it or deny it or seek distraction, so we rationalize that it
doesn't really matter . . . that much.

So, the pounds pile on. Or the debts accumulate. Or sex happens outside of marriage.

All because the concept of delaying pleasure or gratification is completely foreign.

"Delaying what? Never heard of it."

That's very likely true.

***Delayed gratification =
the ability to resist the temptation for an immediate reward and
wait for a later reward.***

Like saying "no" *now* so that WHEN you can say "yes" later, there's no guilt, no baggage, no long-term stuff to deal with.

Decide to save a piece of that decadent dessert for later. Write your name on the plastic-wrap-covered slice and put it in the back of the fridge. Bet it will taste even better then.

Choose to save enough cash to buy that gotta-have new whatever. Post a picture of it on your mirror, dashboard, in your locker—to encourage the penny-pinching that will make it yours sooner. You'll prize the purchase even more by then.

Commit to save sex for your wedding night. Avoid tempting situations and anything that pushes you to compromise, rationalize or just give up.

Surround yourself with encouragement, support and accountability and set yourself up for sex without baggage. For sex the way God designed it.

"But our wedding is only a day . . . "

"a week . . . "

"a month . . . "

"a couple months . . . "

"six months, tops . . . away."

"We're getting married for sure. Really we will. I'm sure of it."

"So what if we move up the 'wedding night'? Does it matter that much?"

"Come on. It's a ceremony and a piece of paper. That's it."

Let me ask you this. **Why are you spending all that time and money for a ceremony?**

Because you want all your friends and family to celebrate the start of your new life together.

Because a vow to spend the rest of your life with someone is a big deal. It's huge and should be cheered in a huge way. And commemorated. And applauded.

And what better way to mark and honor this promise than to save the joining of two bodies as one for the wedding night?

The WHEN of saving sex for marriage understands that I don't have to have *it* right now—in this case sex—just because I want it.

6

Yep, the WHERE matters too

If saving sex for marriage is a priority in your life, you already know the WHERE of anything related to guy/girl relationships matters. Right?

Good. Because it matters sooooo much.

A lot of WHEREs can spell trouble. Like the two of you . . .

- alone and snuggled up in a cozy car. Especially after dark.

- hanging out in bedrooms whether someone's home or not. A huge no-no.

- at make-out, hook-up or hang out parties. These take trouble to a whole new level.

- and of course, let's not forget the parents-are-gone-for-the-weekend situation. Bad. Very bad.

But you already know all this. Because you're smart enough to know, in both your heart and head, that all of the above situations put your commitment to wait for sex in jeopardy. You get it, right?

One or both of you may be thinking,

"What's the big deal if we're home alone?"

Sure, it's possible to find yourselves in a scenario like this and not get in deep trouble, but do you want to take that risk?

You will be sooooo tempted to rationalize—you know, so the situation doesn't look so iffy. So you don't feel so guilty. But look what happens then.

"We'll only kiss a little . . ."

But a couple kisses turn into a lot of kisses.

Soon we're pressed together, stretched out on the couch.

He eases my shirt up. I don't want the amazing kissing to stop.

This is still okay. Isn't it?

Sound familiar?? Or maybe this . . .

"We can handle a little alone time . . . "

I convinced her it would be fine.

Mom and dad would be home soon anyway.

But things got pretty hot pretty fast. Like incredibly fast.

And Mom and Dad didn't come home soon.

"Just because everyone else at the party will be making out, doesn't mean we have to . . . "

"We should leave . . ."

"Nah. Let's stick around a while." His lips brush against my ear, and his arm tugs me closer.

A scan of the room quickens my pulse. Hushed whispers have replaced loud conversations and a slow, romantic song pulses through the house. Snuggling couples are everywhere. Some pretty intense making out is already going on.

"No need to rush home . . ." he whispers as we slide into an empty recliner.

So we stay a little while. What's the harm?

It's time for complete, gut-level honesty.

- Being alone creates an intensely tempting situation.

- It almost never ends with "a little kissing."
- Group settings where the featured activity is making out are no better than being alone.

It's normal to want to get all close and cozy. That's why you have to be extra careful about the WHERE.

✓ Plan WHERE you'll go ahead of time. A "no plan" evening is a recipe for trouble.

✓ Choose double dates OR group activities with others who also want to limit compromising situations.

✓ It's not lame to hang out with Mom, Dad and those young siblings who think you're so cool. A family dinner, movie or game night? The perfect opportunity to be together without the temptations that come with being alone.

✓ Agree not to hang out in the car before, during or after a date. Extend that to bedrooms, too, with no exceptions.

Be smart. Don't ignore the WHERE of saving sex for marriage.

7

WHERE does your mind hang-out?

As the saving sex for marriage cheerleader, I have to insist we discuss another kind of WHERE.

This WHERE is more of a mental WHERE than a physical WHERE.

I bet you spend a fair percentage of each day online, chatting and connecting via Facebook or Twitter, Tumblr, Instagram, or Snapchat. Or any number of other online "hang outs".

You surf for answers to anything you could possibly want to know. Because at your very fingertips lies a limitless amount of information.

You most likely have an online source for music. YouTube or Spotify, Pandora or iTunes. Or maybe you're old school and depend on the old standby, the radio, to get your music fix.

Thanks to technology, the list of places our minds can go is endless. And that's not a bad thing as long as we realize the enormous power these "places" have to mold who we are. To shape our thinking and decision-making skills and impact our morals and values.

Every "place" you choose to spend time will influence your character.

The mindset of your favorite "hang-outs" can't help but seep into your mind, your heart, your soul. Again, that's not a bad thing if you're careful about the WHEREs.

That whole power/influence/seeping can be a positive force, nudging you along on the right path. OR it can drag you in the opposite direction, so fast your head will spin.

The choice of WHERE you go, the influences you let in, those choices belong to you alone.

No one makes you visit inappropriate websites. No one forces you to listen to suggestive music. No one threatens your life if you skip the sexual-innuendo-laden movies and dramas.

And don't for one second argue,

"that stuff doesn't affect me."

That's hogwash, pure and simple. It affects everyone to some degree. You really wanna give it a shot just to see how much it messes with you? I sure hope not.

Your brain has the incredible ability to record, remember and dwell on things. Ever have a catchy advertising slogan stuck in your head for days? No matter how hard you try to get rid of it, it hangs around. The jingle becomes annoying but it's not harmful.

That can't be said about a lot of the stuff out there just waiting for an open door into your mind.

Don't fill your head with stuff that contradicts the way you want to live your life. Rather—

- ✓ **Choose to hang out where the influence will strengthen your values, your character, and yes, your commitment to wait for sex.**
- ✓ **Surround yourself with influences that will make the battle to save sex for marriage easier, not more difficult.**

Because saving sex for marriage matters!

Beth Steury

8

"HOW far is too far?"

When I was in high school, we had these pretty cool Sunday School teachers who said we could write down any question we'd like them to answer. So we banded together and jotted down a most pressing question.

"How far is too far?"

Mostly, as teenagers with very little dating experience, we were okay with the whole no sex before marriage stance. I say mostly because one among us, who was known for pushing every boundary ever put before her, wasn't all that convinced. Anyway, in case the opportunity ever arose, we thought we needed to know what we *could* do. Ya know?

So, we sat on the edge of our seats, waiting for the answer that turned out to be rather generic and intensely disappointing. **Not** the specific line in the sand we sought. It went something like,

"Just don't go so far that you won't be able to stop."

Well, duh.

But how did that help us? Where was the don't-cross-this-line answer we wanted?

We expected and wanted specifics, like, ***"This is okay. But this is not." Something like "Kissing is okay but _____ (fill in the blank) is going too far."***

Make it simple, please, cut and dried, with no gray areas because we don't want to mess this up. NOR do we want to miss out on stuff we *could* be doing. So, thank you very much for settling this important issue for us so we won't have to think too hard about it ourselves.

Except that didn't happen. We were left to figure it out on our own.

***Now*, I get how that was a lot better answer than our teenage minds realized. *Now*, I understand that "the line in the sand" isn't that simple to establish.**

I do not recommend a trial-and-error approach to

discover this mysterious "line". Because if you do that, you might as well start picking out baby names right away.

The fact is, there isn't a magic boundary where anything to the left is A-okay and everything to the right is too far.

You know why? Because the whole *"how far is too far?"* dilemma focuses on the wrong thing entirely.

If you want to save sex for marriage, stop asking "how far?"

Instead, put the emphasis on protecting your commitment to wait. Seeing how close to sex you can get without doing it is not protecting. Again, get out the baby names book because you'll probably be needing it.

I can't tell you where to draw the line. That's a decision you have to make for yourself.

I will say this. Please, oh please, don't be like the little kid whose toes hang over the edge of the cliff as he pushes against the guard rail. That will NOT keep sex

out of your relationship.

But I will give you more than my cool Sunday School teachers gave me and my friends. Some things to consider.

- If the right person's fingers are laced with yours, holding hands sends tingles racing through your entire body.
- Kissing feels amazing as it ignites emotions you never knew existed.
- Making-out will not have you thinking about stopping.
- Bare skin could well mean the death of your no-sex commitment.
- Horizontal positions will jab deep dents in the strongest stance to wait.
- Summer attire can create tempting situations at a moment's notice.
- And there's nothing innocent, okay, or acceptable about showering together.

Instead of searching for the answer to,

"How far is too far?", ask yourself, "What can we do that won't leave us consumed with thoughts of sex?"

Hmm. That might mean dialing things back because you've already passed into dangerous territory. Better to realize it now than later. Maybe just minor kissing is all you can handle or no kissing at all. You may have to draw the line at holding hands. Maybe being alone even a little is going to be too tempting.

Whatever the sacrifice—and yeah, it will feel like a sacrifice, so get prepared—do it anyway. Dig your heels in deep because tomorrow or next week or next month, you'll think of a bunch of reasons why it's okay to go just a little further. Stand firm. Don't rationalize. No compromising. Do not give in.

Saving sex for marriage is WORTH IT.

YOU are worth waiting for.

9

HOW?
No back-up plan

It quickly became a PLAN B kind of day. Nothing was going as expected. By noon plans B, C and D had been abandoned. My only hope at that point was for the day to end before the alphabet did.

I'm an organizer who likes things to go as planned. But experience has taught me the importance of flexibility in the daily-ness of life. Being able to roll with the punches is key because seldom do things go exactly as planned.

But if you're committed to saving sex for marriage, squash ALL thoughts of flexibility. Don't entertain for one second bending or

adjusting your plan. *Not even a little.*

Because there's absolutely no place for a PLAN B or C or D when it comes to saving sex for marriage.

Whatever you do, do not even discuss a back-up plan. Refuse to consider a PLAN B or C or D—no matter how small the adjustment may seem. Don't do it.

The mere mention of a BACK-UP PLAN will do the opposite of PROTECT your commitment. It will wreak havoc with it.

Banish to some remote planet the mere whisper of anything that resembles backing down. You know like, keeping a stash of condoms in your purse, wallet, or car for "just in case." Or getting a prescription for birth-control pills—to help regulate your periods, of course—with the unmentioned benefit of protection should you slip-up.

Do not give yourself an out. *No. No. No.*

Forget flexibility but please do get familiar with his close cousin, ***resourcefulness.*** When the doubts, questions and intense feelings hit, the ones you aren't as prepared for as you thought you would be, it'll be tempting to just throw in the towel.

The most thought-out approach to waiting, surrounded by the best of intentions, will be tested. You can count on it. It will happen.

One or both of you, at some point, will say or at the very least think—

> *"I didn't know being in a relationship with you would feel like this."*

"I had no clue our connection would be so strong."

"Waiting for marriage is taking too long."

"I just can't wait any longer . . . "

*"It's hopeless. Might as well just give up. Either that or stop seeing each other. Which we **aren't** going to do."*

When that happens, step back and take a breath.

You don't have to end the relationship. There are other options.

It's time to get resourceful and look for ways to be together without being alone.

✓ A BBQ with the family.

✓ Take Mom and Dad to a movie with you.

- ✓ Go to every church event on the calendar.
- ✓ Stick close to friends also committed to no sex.
- ✓ Babysit the sibs—the ones old enough to tell on you if there's any hanky-panky.
- ✓ Volunteer as a couple to coach a kids' sports team or help the elderly neighbor. Serve at the soup kitchen or do yard work for the local shelter. *Whatever.*

Getting involved in worthwhile pursuits will grow your relationship in a positive way. And less alone time will reign in the physical temptations. A win-win situation.

1. **Remind yourselves why you committed to waiting.**
2. **Seek accountability from both peers and a trusted mentor.**
3. **Reinforce the steps you've used in the past to protect your commitment.**

**Saving sex for marriage is worth the effort it takes.
Don't even think back-up plan.**

10

WHY save sex for marriage?

If there were just one reason to save sex for marriage, this chapter would be easy to write. Oh, so easy to write. Bam… In CAPS with an extra bold font I'd state the one reason. Expound, explore and elaborate on that one reason and that would be it.

But that's not the case.

There are so many reasons to wait for the commitment of marriage to share your body—and your heart and soul—with another person.

Where do I begin? Which reason do I start with?

Begin . . . *start with*.

Ah ha. I think I've answered my own questions.

Here's what I said back when this series began:

> **"I believe that sex is an amazing gift God created for one man and one woman, committed to each other in marriage, to share for the rest of their lives."**

The first WHY of saving sex for marriage has to be this: GOD who created sex says that only when a man and a woman have made a lifetime commitment to each other, before GOD, their family and friends, should they allow themselves the pleasure of sex.

The creator—***the guy who invented sex***—said that.

Hold that very important thought for a moment.

We recently bought a new washing machine. A state-of-the-art laundry system no less, to replace our thirty-year-old trusty relic. As the old machine and the fancy new one had little in common, the need to keep the new machine's owner's manual very near became apparent five seconds after the installation guys left.

Yeah, right, you say. It's a washing machine—no big deal. Throw in the dirty stuff, dump in some detergent, push the ON button. Later take out the clean stuff. Piece of cake, right?

So not right. It's just a washing machine, yeah, but

it's much more complicated than that.

And since it was pretty expensive, we don't want to you know, destroy it. The number of WARNING notices throughout the manual drove home the need to use the machine properly lest we find ourselves purchasing another laundry system in the not-too-distant future.

It requires frequent "cleaning"—I guess so it can then "clean" our clothes. I'm constantly digging out that owner's manual to be sure I use the techniques recommended by the manufacturer. You know, ***the creator of the machine***, whom I must trust to know the best way to keep my new laundry system performing at its peak.

Pretty much like the way the *creator of sex* knows what's best when it comes to sex. HIS recommendation? Life-long, exclusive commitment to one husband or wife in marriage.

Maybe you have a difficult time with GOD and sex mentioned in the same sentence. Or paragraph even. I get that. Our society has so trampled on the sacredness of sex, dragging it through the gutter at every opportunity, that it's easy to forget the whole thing was GOD's idea from the beginning. If you have doubts about that statement, think about this.

Sex is way too good to have occurred by accident.

As in NO one created it, it just so happens that it works. I don't think so.

If the creator of sex advises this intimate act be saved for marriage, shouldn't we listen?

If decisions in the past led you away from waiting, you can commit from today on to wait. I will say it until my dying breath:

it's never too late to choose to save future sexual experiences for marriage

One sexual partner or a hundred—it doesn't matter. Don't keep repeating past mistakes. **You can chart a new course. You can head in a new direction.**

Whether you've always been committed to waiting OR you're venturing into new territory, remember the first reason to save sex—or future sexual experiences—for marriage **comes from the creator himself.**

11

WHY?
Do you know where babies come from?

Oh, yeah, I remember. *Sex.* That's where babies come from.

"Well, duh. Everyone knows that."

Hmm. Really, do they? Because there's a whole lot of sex happening between people who do not want a baby, who have no way to provide for a baby. Guys and girls who haven't a clue if their connection to each other might last to see the birth of the child their actions may create.

"But we're careful—we use birth control."

No form of birth control is 100% effective even when used properly every single time.

Let me ask you this. Have you given one thought to think how an unplanned pregnancy would affect your life? Your partner's life? Your plans for the future? Your partner's plans for the future?

"If I get pregnant/she gets pregnant, we'll figure it out."

Excuse me, but that's it?? You'll figure it out???

A pregnancy will affect every day of the rest of your lives. Every minute of every day. Absolutely nothing changes your world like becoming a parent.

Babies are sweet and cute and precious. Without a doubt.

But babies require huge amounts of time and money and energy and wisdom. Boy, do they.

Bottom line: Lots and lots of people haven't given nearly enough thought to the fact that the physical intimacy they are or want to be engaging in has the potential to create a life.

Sex exists for two very specific reasons. To create a deep and lasting bond between two people committed to a lifetime together and to make babies.

Because we have nothing better to do OR need to explore how we really feel about each other are not mentioned. Anywhere.

Think about it. Doesn't the act that creates a new life deserve mega amounts of respect? Shouldn't it be approached with caution and reverence and only after a marriage commitment?

When you're tempted to lower your standards and back out of your commitment to save sex— or future sexual experiences—for marriage, ask yourself this: Am I in a position to raise a child?

Saving sex for marriage will eliminate the risk of pregnancy before marriage.

Another important reason WHY it makes sense to wait.

12

WHY?
The facts and fiction about STDs

First some facts. According to the Centers for Disease Control (CDC), there are more than 20 types of STDs that cause nearly 20 million new cases of sexually transmitted diseases (STD) each year.

Half of these new infections are among young people ages 15 to 24. STDs affect men and women of all backgrounds and economic levels.

Talk about a scary epidemic.

Now for some of the myths.

1. **"I trust the guy/girl I'm seeing, so worrying about STDs isn't necessary."** Maybe you think the relationship has reached a level of trust that assures he/she would tell you if there was cause to worry. But he/she may have no symptoms at all and have no idea they've contracted an STD. You must also consider that the fear a confession will end the relationship might convince someone with a confirmed diagnosis to hide the truth. You know, hoping against hope that the infection won't be passed along. **Trust does not equal safety.**

2. **"Anyway, I'll be able to tell if he/she has an STD."** Not so. At all. Looking at, sniffing around, or sifting through all you know about the person will not confirm or deny an STD. Handsome and muscled? Gorgeous and feminine? The picture of perfect health? None of that is a guarantee. **Only a test can confirm the absence or presence of an STD.**

3. **"We're both virgins so it's impossible for either of us to have**

an STD." Unfortunately, that's not a guarantee either. Maybe neither of you have had actual sexual intercourse, but if either of you have engaged in oral sex or intimacy that stopped just short of intercourse, it's possible to have contracted an STD. **Without a test you can't be sure.**

It almost seems impossible to even fathom but consider with me for a minute. *What if no one in the history of mankind ever had sex with anyone except his/her spouse.* **No premarital sex, no extramarital sex. Only married couples having sex with their spouse.**

I have very serious doubts that STDs would exist at all. And wouldn't that be completely amazing? Of course that's not our reality. Not even close.

So, we're left with the very gripping reality that a myriad of sexually transmitted diseases have infected millions of people, creating a host of medical issues, some of which will last a lifetime. Not to mention the complications for future romantic relationships and marriages.

If you have the slightest inkling you may have contracted a sexually transmitted disease, get tested and seek treatment.

If your past contains one or more sexual partners, whether it seems necessary or not, why not get tested? If you're disease-free, awesome. Keep it that way by saying "NO" to any kind of sexual involvement. If you're not disease-free, get the needed treatment and choose to pursue "renewed waiting"—no further sexual activity, of any kind, until marriage.

> **Remove yourself from the risks that expose you to STDs.**
>
> **Protect your health. Protect your future.**
>
> **Protect the health and future of your someday spouse.**

Another one of the many reasons WHY sex should be saved for marriage.

13

WHY wait?
It's all about the bonding

Do you understand the bonding that happens when two people have sex? If not, then you don't really *get* what sex is all about. That one of the primary purposes of sex is to create a strong and lasting BOND. A 'til-death-do-us-part kind of connection.

In case you think it's just us religious kinds who go on about the whole bonding thing, science has proven it really does exist. Here's how it works.

During physical contact, a woman's brain releases the hormone oxytocin—sometimes called the "cuddle hormone"—which produces feelings of closeness, trust, and yes, *bonding*. During sex oxytocin floods the brain causing the desire for this awesome experience to happen again. This same hormone is present at the onset of labor and during breastfeeding, again, to create a bond—this time between a mother and her newborn baby.

Close contact and physical intimacy cause a man's brain to secrete the hormone vasopressin—known as the "monogamy hormone". As in committed to one person—that's what monogamy means. It triggers a feeling of attachment to the woman he's intimately involved with and later also aids in bonding a father to his children.

Both men and women's brains produce addictive doses of the pleasure hormone dopamine during physical intimacy. Known as the "feel good" or "reward" hormone, dopamine rages through the brain with an intense sensation of energy and exhilaration. It initiates a need and/or desire to repeat the sexual experiences.

Closeness. Trust. Attachment. Totally awesome, even crucial, in a marriage relationship. Key ingredients to a strong marriage, for sure.

But maybe not so great in a dating relationship. Because if this hormone-induced trust and attachment happens too soon, it almost always spells trouble, sometimes even disaster.

For one, wise decision making flies out the window in favor of more sex. And then this glue-like connection created by the sex messes with a person's judgment, often keeping him/her in a relationship that needs to end.

And if we're talking about a casual hook-up or one-night stand? **Wow.** A flood of bonding hormones in that situation is a *really, really bad idea.*

The thing you have to understand is these amazingly awesome hormones can't distinguish between a hook-up and a lifelong soul mate.

Triggered by any physical intimacy, they get down to business regardless of the realities of the relationship. *Even if there's not a relationship at all.*

This whole chemical process creates an adhesive effect, like really sticky glue. Again, an amazing thing in a marriage. The bonds created by these raging hormones are meant to keep a couple together through thick and thin, the good times and the really rotten stuff. Through all the years of sharing a life.

But rip these glued-together persons apart when they go their separate ways in a couple weeks, months or years, and we're talking major devastation. Deeply

emotional, gut-wrenching pain.

Repeated bonding and ripping apart messes with the brain's ability to create lasting connections. Which completely blows holes in the I'll-settle-down-when-I'm-done-having-fun theory.

Treating sex with such a casual attitude doesn't make it a casual experience. It was never intended to be the no-strings-attached encounter so many people want to make it.

If all this doesn't convince you that the design for sex was for the lifelong commitment of marriage, then *what will convince you?*

BUT I ALREADY DIDN'T WAIT!!

You and a bunch of other people, too. Well, you can't change the past. But you can learn from it. And you sure as heck don't have to repeat it.

Now that you understand the whole brain sex connection, would you even consider joining your body with anyone to whom you're not married?

Stop buying the lies that sex equals love and that everyone else is doing it.

Or that you can't change your ways and/or that it really doesn't matter anyway.

That you don't deserve more and better.

Because you do deserve better.

Your choices about sex DO matter. They matter sooo very much.

If bonding and breaking up—whether it be once or fifty times—has left you scarred and hurting, wondering where to go from here, stop, take a deep breath, and allow yourself to believe this important truth—

your past does not have to make the decisions for your future.

You can start over. Choose a different path. Make better, wiser decisions.

- ✓ Distance yourself from all physically intimate relationships.
- ✓ Take some time to evaluate your life.
- ✓ But don't go it alone.
- ✓ Seek the support of a friend, parent, teacher, pastor, coach—someone with whom you can be totally honest. Someone who can walk along this new path with you.

Premarital sex often leaves baggage in the form of low self-esteem, confusion, depression, and a host of other mental and emotional issues.

If past choices are interfering with living your life, seek professional help from a counselor, a nurse, a doctor, a minister. If the thought of suicide even whispers through your brain, tell someone immediately. Please don't let past mistakes rob you of a promising future.

Now that you understand WHAT sex is all about, you'll want to save all, or any additional sexual experiences, for your future spouse.

Save those amazing, bonding hormones for the right time and place, *marriage*.

Because you are worth waiting for.

More in the "Waiting Matters" Series . . . available now in paperback and ebook.

saving sex for marriage in a Fifty Shades world

Coming soon . . .

but I didn't wait

Check out the "Choices Matter" Series book #1 available now in paperback and ebook.

before I knew you

After a series of bad choices rocked his world, seventeen-year-old Preston charts a new course as far from his ladies' man ways as he can get. Then he meets Maggie, the new girl in town on the first day of their junior year. She's beautiful on the inside and out, knows nothing of his past, and he can't get her out of his mind.

After a disastrous first date leaves her skeptical about the guys at Madison High, Maggie slows down her pursuit of a guy to trust with her white-wedding-dress future. He'd have to be nothing like the jerk who forced her first kiss. Someone more like Preston, who's been nothing but sweet and helpful. But he is so out of her league.

Will Preston's past jeopardize his chances with the new girl? Can Maggie afford to let her guard down around the charming Preston?

Preston and Maggie's story continues in books 2 & 3 in the "Choices Matter" series.

Coming soon in paperback and ebook!

because I know you

between you and me

ABOUT THE AUTHOR

Beth immerses herself in the world of YA via substitute teaching, by connecting with the teenage staff and patrons at the fast food joint where she claims the back booth as her office, and by reading YA fiction.

She welcomes questions and topic suggestions on the *"Waiting Matters ... Because YOU Matter"* blog that inspired the Waiting Matters books. Write to her at waitingmatters@gmail.com.

Check out her *Choices Matter* series that follows Preston and Maggie as they navigate the choppy waters of high school and guy/girl relationships.

Connect with Beth at BethSteury.com for all the news on upcoming releases. Find her on Facebook at BethSteury, Author; on Twitter @Beth_Steury; and on Instagram and Goodreads.

Made in the USA
Lexington, KY
24 September 2019